Designed to be Home: Professionally Designed Spaces and the Real Families That Call Them Home
by Harmony Weihs with Kate Savitch

Published by designHARMONY:
11251 120TH Avenue NE, suite #201, Kirkland, WA 98033
www.designharmonyinfo.com
instagram: designharmonyinsta

Book formatting by Nikki Easterday
Floor plans by Margaret Bouniol

Professional Photographs © 2016 Holland Photography by Cory Holland. Used by permission. All rights reserved.
Everyday Photographs © 2016 Harmony Weihs. All rights reserved.

ISBN: 978-0-692-78588-1

Printed in the United States of America

For Kate, the best business partner, friend, listener, mama and hardest working person I know. Without you I may not have made it through this last year…

…and for my top two designs to date, Holden and Emma.

- Harmony

the WHO the WHAT the WHERE

INTERIOR DESIGNS / WRITING / CREATIVE DESIGN
harmony weihs

PROJECT CONCEPT / EDITOR / PUBLISHER
kate savitch

PROFESSIONAL DESIGN PHOTOS
cory holland

EVERYDAY CLIENT PHOTOS
harmony's iPhone 6S+

LAYOUT DESIGN
nikki easterday

PRINTED
United States of America

eternally GRATEFUL

How do you repay the people who allow you to do what you love everyday and trust you even when they often have no idea what you are talking about?

I wish I had the answer.

Our clients are our hall pass and literally give us their keys.

I am humbled that most of our clients are return customers, and to that I am speechless. I do not think I could do what you do...here is my key, my credit card, yeah sure, make a ton of noise and create a constant settling of dust while I am trying to make dinner. Have at it, get it done and I "hope" I like the result you have communicated or what...

...we start over?

TRUST at the utmost level.

Thank you does not even begin to express how I feel toward all of you. From the bottom of my heart, thank you.

I am eternally grateful.

note to READERS

This is not another book about teaching you design, where to place your furniture or a lesson in balancing color.

This is about our clients, the real families who call the designs home.

It's about the families that invite us not only into their homes but also into their lives. We help when spouses cannot see eye to eye, where to splurge and where to save.

Design is personal.
Often very personal.

We are in their homes for months at a time. We meet their extended families. We see them in their bathrobes early in the morning and with a glass of wine in the evening. We get to know them, their children, their pets and the things that make them unique. We learn about what they've been through and what they are going through. It is a privilege and a gift to be welcomed into their homes and for us to show you, the reader, how the designs come to life with the real people who live there.

So often we flip through a magazine or visit an interior design site and see these gorgeous rooms; they are staged to perfection. Believe me, we sweat over the details. Is the chair at the right angle? Are the flowers the right scale? It is what we call the "final design" in all it's glory before anyone steps foot, spills a drop of red wine or puts a stack of bills and school calendars on the counter. Professionally shot designs are far from everyday life and how people live on a daily basis, including me.

Let's get real. We will show you the beautiful, picture perfect designs I had in my head in contrast to seeing the real families, how they live and use the rooms on a daily basis. I believe that the designs have no meaning without the families who call them home. Because at the end of the day my biggest passion and goal is to create a space where the families love being and make loads of memories together.

the EVERYDAY

The real families in their everyday lives, what
makes the designs unique and meaningful to them.

the BEAUTY

Our professional after photos staged
exactly how I envisioned the designs to be.

the BEGINNING

I was not an A student, far from it. I did not excel at pen to paper, test taking or reading books in anything other than the pace of a young tortoise. Spelling, don't even get me started.

Simple math.
Thank goodness for calculators.

I did, however, excel in all things creative, visual and hands on. The principal at my high school allowed me to paint a mural on the wall, so I was doing something right in that department.

I grew up with a father who had a successful business as a custom home builder. Not only did I learn the difference between good and great construction and finishing, I saw my father home every day at 5:00 pm and present in our lives. Being the middle of three girls, my mother not only keep the estrogen ship afloat by taking care of our every needs, she helped make all the agonizing decisions that go along with building a home {which they did together a half dozen times}.

You could say I was destined to end up at yet another construction site with a tape measure in hand.

Moving from my beautiful, lush valley hometown of Corvallis, OR to a skyscraper-filled Seattle with Blue Angles flying overhead.

I soon found myself sitting in a classroom doing what I thrived at and it was like nothing I had ever felt to date. I was great at dreaming but even better at executing. There was no looking back.

Graduating from the Art Institute of Seattle in 1997 with an AAA in Apparel Design. I quickly landed a job on career day and was off-to-the-races designing and developing bags and apparel, flying from Seattle to Asia regularly and loving every minute of it. One job lead to the next in the small Seattle athletic apparel companies that I felt so connected to. After about a decade, I started to feel stagnate, unchallenged and very, very far removed from the people wearing the yoga pants, running jackets and mountaineering base layers I was designing.

I wanted to be closer to the end user of my designs.

I wanted to feel excited about what I was creating, to grow and to be challenged. I wanted to be outside on those rare sunny Seattle days and have some say in what defined work hours and balance of life. I wanted something more than the cubical corporate world; and to set out on my own.

It was a big risk, it was scary, but I believe that are best opportunities to grow are when we are the most uncomfortable.

So, in 2006 I started my company, designHARMONY as a full time freelance designer for apparel and interiors. Although my schooling was for apparel design the general concepts applied when transitioning into interiors. With that said, I jumped two feet into a completely new industry with little knowledge of where to start. It was thrilling at times and constantly overwhelming but I got my wish, I was excited about design again. Finally I was challenged and learning every day. Learning so much in fact I often found it very hard to get some shuteye.

In about 2010 I was designing about fifty percent apparel/bags and fifty percent interiors. I was newly married, working out of our home office when our son Holden arrived in 2011. One interior job lead to the next, and the next, and quickly I was busy.

Very busy.

I often thought about where I wanted to take my company of one. I knew I never wanted to be a large design firm as that would require strict hours, a dress code other than yoga pants {when not seeing clients} and probably more headaches than it was worth. I came to a point where I either had to start turning down a lot of work or get help.

Over the next few years I had some great people who worked with me part time. In the end I knew if I was going to add someone to my business full time it had to be the right person. Not necessarily someone who knew the specific industry but somebody who was all in, invested and dreamt big. So I kept searching in hopes of finding the right person.

In 2014 I was struggling getting pregnant for the second time. I was in and out of fertility appointments. At the same time, my business was flourishing and I could not take my company to the next level without help. It was a trying time to say the least.

Out of the blue, I received an email from Kate Savitch. She and her husband just built a home in Kirkland and she fell in love with interiors and wanted to get into the field. Kate had a full time career but was feeling stagnant.

The morning Kate and I met for the first time, I had just found out I was not pregnant after trying for a year and a half. I was in a state of emotional rawness but I dragged myself there, looking oh so professional in my Seahawks sweatshirt and flip flops. I knew from that moment Kate was the person I was searching for. Sometimes you just know.

Kate meant business.

I knew that if Kate was to come on board I did not want to teach her design so we would be doing the same thing. I wanted us to specialize in different areas. Kate's background in client service and marketing was perfect for working with clients and attention to detail it takes to make the designs come to life.

A few months later I was expecting (yeah!) and we were quickly outgrowing our home offices. Kate also just had her second child so we were on our last leg of our home offices actually working well. My daughter Emma arrived in October of 2014 and I took off 3 months to do the truly most important job, being a mama. We knew it was time to open up a small design studio. We moved fast in the next six weeks to design and customize our new space to meet our needs for the next phase of our business.

Do you hear that?
Silence.

And there you have it, the designHARMONY Studio was born. It's a blissful place where we can focus on our clients, be creative and are able to go home and completely shut off in this 24/7 tech age. We are now a corporation of two. You read that right, a corporation of two.

Currently, I create the designs and Kate executes every last detail to a tee. It has worked out exceptionally well and could think of no one else I would rather partner with.

Kate had this concept.

Briskly walking into the studio as if casually talking about how she takes her coffee she said, "we're writing a coffee table book". I looked over at her after absorbing this grandiose concept, and she was off typing away, putting out fires and taking calls. I could not sleep for weeks. I was excited.

A design book? The last thing I wanted to do was add to the forever-bulging interior design section of "my home will never look that perfect" or "who the heck actually LIVES there?" If we set out to write a book it had to be different.

It had to be personal.

If it was not personal we would be like everyone else. Showing beautiful perfection without any of the truth or depth that mattered. And here we are, thanks to Kate.

the DESIGN PHILOSOPHY

I live, breathe and dream design. It is part of my DNA.

But what is design? To me design is not what something looks like but how it makes you feel. I believe that a great design does not flaunt her features but instead whispers them. Often times people have a hard time articulating what it is they like about a space because it's not one thing. It's all encompassing.

It is the feeling they get from being in the space.

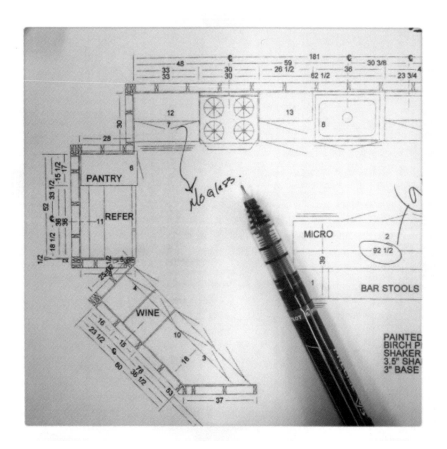

Things have to have FORM + FUNCTION. But what does that mean really? To me it means you, the person pulling out their credit card, has to love how everything looks. The design has to function for what you need it to do. If something looks beautiful but is terribly uncomfortable, or falls over every time you touch it, to me it is a bad design.

I strive to build character and to create a bit of a soul in my designs. So often we look at a magazine or a design blog and it's no doubt beautiful but lacks character. One of the most important things to me is creating elements within the designs that have meaning to the people I am designing for. Without that I feel it is hollow and can often feel a bit artificial.

RECLAIMED

In my past career I worked in the world of design it here, build it overseas and ship it back home. Something about that felt so far removed and unsupportive of all the amazing talented people we have at our doorstep. I now bask in the opportunity to work with local craftspeople. Seeing someone take a concept, whether it is a piece of art, a table or custom drapery, and make it come to life, is magical. It is seldom less expensive but I can guarantee it will last longer and have a much deeper meaning.

I am passionate about reclaiming and refurbishing materials to add character and provide a sustainable alternative to buying new. By using reclaimed materials or repurposing something outdated, there is a unique story behind every piece.

I jump on the chance to repurpose a family heirloom. I love hunting through architectural salvage yards and being inspired by something from the past, only to give it a second chance. Without these unique elements, I feel design can feel too manufactured and mass produced. The last thing I want for my clients' home is it to feel like a furniture showroom with no connection to who they are, how they live and what is most important to them.

CUSTOM

What does that even mean really? Custom to me means unique to you and one-of-a-kind. Sometimes people get scared of the word custom, thinking it will be astronomical in cost. In reality it does not have to be.

All of our clients have different goals within their designs and we can often find what we need at retail stores or at the Seattle Design Center. When we cannot, or when I feel retail will not do the space justice, we go custom. I typically will suggest a minimum of one custom element that is unique to the clients and their home within each design.

Retail can have a lot of great options. The downside sometimes is that you are limited to what they offer at that moment in time, to "standard" measurements of pieces. When we design something custom it will often fit much better in the space and we are not limited to the sizes, colors, shapes and details that retailers offer.

Much like our reclaimed + repurposed pieces, with custom projects we are able to support local craftspeople which is something very dear to my heart.

our NEIGHBORHOOD

We are the Evergreen state. The Emerald City. We are made up of endless year round green trees, snowcapped volcanoes and big bodies of water. And why yes, we have lots and lots of drizzly rain with an often constant dose of gray skies. We pride ourselves on our boutique coffee shops around every corner, our ever growing tech industry, ground breaking scientists, 2-day delivery packages at our doorsteps and our love for the outdoors.

We are a hub of craft microbreweries, wineries, standout local restaurants and of course phenomenal music. We have been known to pack a few stadiums and break sound records.

We recycle.
Everything.

Companies like Microsoft, Amazon, Nordstrom, Boeing, Starbucks, REI, Costco and Weyerhaeuser to name a few, were founded here and most are still thriving here. Hendrix, Nirvana, Sir-Mix-A lot, Heart, Pearl Jam, Soundgarden and Macklemore have kept us singing for years.

Supporting our local farmers and artisans is our passion. You will often spot flying fish in our beloved Pike Place Market, one of the oldest continuously operated public farmers' markets in the country.

Sitting between the magnificent Olympic + Cascade mountain ranges we are always struck by the sight of Mount Rainier, one of the largest, most glaciated peaks in the lower 48. Proud to say our Jim Whittaker was the first American to summit a little mountain called Everest, back in '63.

We never take the sun for granted and bask in it when and wherever. When 61 degrees hits we are outside with shorts, sunscreen in hand, soaking it all in. When it is raining in the city, snow is covering our mountain tops and we are hitting the slopes.

Want to look like a local? Leave your umbrella at home.

We live for comfort, often too much. We forget it is not common in other parts of the country to wear a tee shirt and jeans to a 5 star restaurant. It is a love hate relationship. Casual is good but maybe we have taken it one sock and sandal step too far.

The outdoors is our backyard.

COME PLAY WITH US.

the HOMES

the DESIGNS

elevated architecture   NOOK + OFFICE   p28

elevated architecture   DINING ROOM   p42

elevated architecture   GREAT ROOM   p54

instrumental elements   MUSIC + LIBRARY   p68

house that love built   ENTRY   p82

house that love built   GREAT ROOM   p90

truly tranquil   MASTER BATH   p102

east meets west   ENTRY   p114

dudes dwelling   DINING ROOM   p130

raise the roof   KITCHEN   p166

home away from home   MASTER BATH   p186

home away from home   OFFICE + LAUNDRY   p196

country culinary   KITCHEN   p208

salvaged for perspective   GREAT ROOM   p220

salvaged for perspective   OFFICE   p232

reclaimed space   KITCHEN   p246

technically serene   ENTRY   p264

technically serene   GUEST ROOM   p274

technically serene   DINING ROOM   p280

technically serene   FAMILY ROOM   p294

elevated architecture

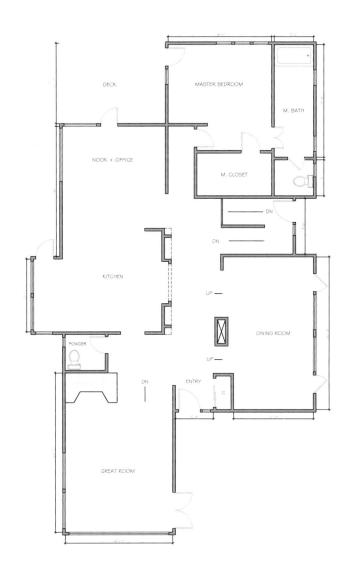

the HOUSE

kenmore, WA

built in 1986

3,340 SF

3 bed / 2.5 bath

custom pacific NW

the FAMILY

PETER / software engineer;
video games

ANGELA / business executive +
community volunteer

LIAM / 6 years

MEI LI / 4 years

SW 7619 | Labradorite

elevated architecture

_____

NOOK + OFFICE

the WANTS the WISHES

Peter + Angela were one of my first clients who trusted me with a top to bottom full room design. I was in total awe of their stunning custom home, which was originally designed by a local architect. I knew this was not another house on the block. I was honored to be a part of making it their home while getting to know their family. Peter + Angela were tired of throwaway furniture and wanted quality pieces that would grow with their family. They wanted a comfortable space that could seat their family for casual meals, a working office that looked presentable when guests were visiting and storage in which they could hide the school calendars and day-to-day items. The only furniture that was currently in the room was the kids table and chairs. Seeing as breakfast for four worked better for Liam and Mei Li at that scale, it was time to upgrade.

"This space is really intimate and physically brings us close
to each other for end of day conversations or story telling"

As a family they often eat weekend breakfasts and lunches in the nook. Angie likes to read while lounging on the pillows with a cup of coffee and enjoying a break from their busy lives. Liam and Mei Li love jumping into this space and doing everything from school work to reading. On a sunny breezy day, this room is one of their favorites in their home. They open up the windows, let the air blow through, and lean their feet up on the cushions connecting with each other.

I since have designed three other rooms for them and I am ecstatic every time I am asked back. If only I could bottle the expression of excitement on Peter's face on design day I would never have to interview again.

Peter + Angela's home has incredible exposed roof trusses and vaulted ceilings that make their home unique. With such high ceilings a space can often feel cold or has a lack of coziness to it. The correct scale of furniture and art was critical in this corner, as we needed a space for both of them while not blocking the flow to the deck. They wanted a space with custom art to fill the tall wall.

The office is where you can find Angie most evenings finishing up end of day tasks for their family. She loves her custom desk and overhead cabinets that allow her to spread out all of her work, bills and kids artwork that needs sorting.

the BEAUTY

RECLAIMED

When trying to make a 'his' + 'hers' workspace I wanted the areas to still be connected. I did not want it to feel cookie cutter but instead unique to each of them. For Peter's desk we had a clean modern custom desk made of reclaimed fir from a local woodworker. For Angela's desk we sourced reclaimed stair spindles from one of my favorite architectural salvage shops in SODO and had her desk custom built to fit the scale of the space.

Peter's desk rests on top of Angela's as they meet in the corner and are connected while still being unique to their styles. This is by far my favorite design element in the room.

elevated architecture

DINING ROOM

the WANTS the WISHES

It was a joyful day when a received an email from Angie asking for help with their dining room, I could not wait to work with them again. This space was insanely cool. Yet again, I had a blank canvas to work with and the room was large enough to create three zones. They asked for something elegant yet functional that could seat up to eight people. I loved Peter + Angela's request for a live edge table for 8+. It seemed fitting to use maple, a native wood which also ties in nicely with the architecture of their home.

the EVERYDAY

Rumor has it the family receives the most compliments on their dining room than any other space. My guess is because it is not the typical formal dining room that is tucked away in a corner far from the kitchen. Since everyone ends up hanging out in the kitchen, it can be rare we actually use our dining rooms. By making their space casual it makes it more usable. They don't have dinner here on busy weekday evenings so when they slow down and eat here it feels like a treat as if they are out to a special family meal.

I designed the space to have an intimate lounge area by adding custom wall woodwork to bring down the tall ceilings, warm leather chairs and a reclaimed locally built table. This is Angie's mother's favorite space when she visits to enjoy a cup of coffee and read for hours.

the BEAUTY

CUSTOM

Wine storage and a space to spread out was a must for when they host larger groups. We all agree that our favorite element in the room is the custom cabinet designed to look like a library card catalog instead of a predictable standard buffet. Our local cabinetmaker did such a beautiful job of executing the design. What appears to be small drawers is actually one large door for functional storage. This is why I love design and supporting local craftspeople. I have the opportunity to come up with something different. We are able to work with small companies and have face-to-face experiences with them. On the day of install I was ecstatic, it was better than the design in my head as it was built with love.

elevated architecture
_____

GREAT ROOM

the WANTS the WISHES

      Onto room number three! This room is stunning. My four year old could have designed it and the room would have looked astonishing. The bones of it, the architecture and all the beautiful wood windows are to die for. He was at preschool so I decided to take on the task.

      As with their other rooms, they wanted something beautiful yet functional. They needed furniture that could house Liam's + Mei Li's toys when not in use and be a grown up room when the kids were sound asleep. Lots of seating was needed which seems easy enough, I mean the room looks huge!

It is not.

      The footprint is actually quite small, tall ceilings have a way of making us feel as though the room is much larger than it appears. This is one of the main reasons I say in many client consults, "if we do this, it will draw your eye up, make the room feel taller, bigger". Suggesting the right scale of pieces was critical in the success of this room. Multiple focal points always make it challenging… do we focus on the view, the fireplace or the TV?

      How about all three?

the EVERYDAY

"Liam + Mei Li love to jump from one piece of furniture to the next, avoiding the "hot lava" while constantly giggling."

While mom and dad are busy making dinner in ears reach, Liam and Mei Li are busy building tracks and playing to their hearts content. By widening the stairs and tweaking the fireplace we created better flow into the room allowing for a large console that keeps all the toys hidden when not in use. It is where they go on fall and winter nights to light a fire and watch movies and read books together.

the BEAUTY

instrumental elements

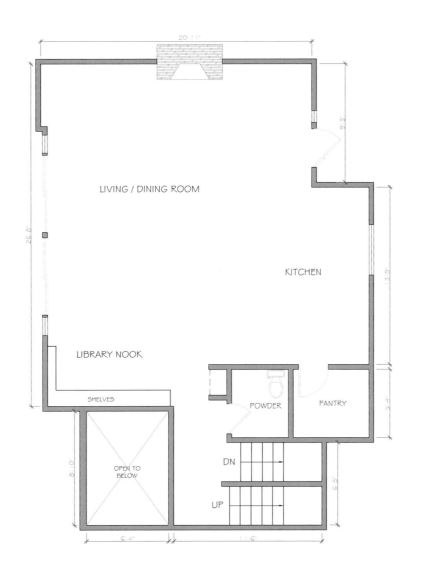

LIVING / DINING ROOM

KITCHEN

LIBRARY NOOK

SHELVES

POWDER

PANTRY

OPEN TO
BELOW

DN

UP

the HOUSE

redmond, WA

built in 2011

1,945 SF

3 bed / 2.5 bath

NW contemporary

the FAMILY

LARRY / software engineer

ERICA / teacher; music specialist

instrumental elements

MUSIC + LIBRARY

the WANTS the WISHES

    I first met Larry + Erica in their apartment they were about to move out of into their newly built home. They had not planned on moving, or even to buy again, but they fell in love with this unique floor plan backing up to a year round northwest greenbelt. I got a sense of their styles, the things that make them special and they were so easy to collaborate with. They finally got their keys and were elated to be the first owners of a new construction house. Although they loved the great room concept they did not want a formal dining space that the large empty corner was intended for. We wanted the area to have a purpose for the things that have had meaning to them and how they live.

    It was staring at me from the other side of the great room. A large, beautiful bass, sadly sitting on its stand, no spot lights, just on it's own. As if screaming, "do something with me, make me a star already!". Nobody puts baby in the corner, as we all know. So we let the big girl shine and I designed a massive bookshelf that focused on Larry's bass and turned it into a piece of art {when not doing her main job, making music of course...}

the EVERYDAY

"While thoroughly integrated into the overall feel of the great room, the library corner also feels separate enough to allow us a sense of comfortable intimacy."

Erica, a music teacher, puts most readers to shame. This girl has ever-growing bookshelves lining most of the corners in their home. The two of them have the most sentimental and loved collections I have seen in years. How could we not focus on what has meaning to them? It is the perfect spot for Larry to unwind and listen to his favorite music. Larry + Erica have been some of my most loyal clients, moving from one project to the next. This by far is my most favorite as it celebrates who they are.

the BEAUTY

CUSTOM

No dining room? But where do they eat? The thing is they prefer to have casual meals together at their kitchen peninsula and hosting large dinner parties was not on their agenda. A couple of times a year they have family in town and did want a proper dining table. Designing custom pieces and seeing them come to life makes me tick. This is no exception. Day-to-day while engrossed in her favorite book it's Erica's sidekick holding her coffee in the am and her Vino Verde at night.

Give the table a few turns, add two half moon leaves and voila, you have a dining table for four. Who wouldn't want to spread brie on a crostini surrounded by LPs and books for days? Oh yea, and baby.

house that love built

featured on **HGTV** ◫ **houzz** ✿ apartment therapy

GREAT ROOM   DINING ROOM   KITCHEN

UP

DN

PANTRY

BATH

C   C

OFFICE

GARAGE

the HOUSE

sammamish, WA
(yea, it's a real town)

built in 2014

3,800 SF

4 bed + office / 4 bath

NW contemporary

the FAMILY

MIKE / business controller

BRANDON / 7 years

house that love built

———————————

ENTRY

the WANTS the WISHES

It was another busy day at work. My inbox was full. I was behind on everything and I had a potential client requesting to meet in person prior to my standard Initial Consultation. This was rarely something I did. Being such a small company (company of 1 back then), you tend to take on jobs where people are ready to go; yesterday. He wanted to take the time to see if I was a good fit for his project. We met at a local coffee shop and he was well prepared. Mike was a young, professional businessman who meant business and asked all of the right questions.

Then my heart sank, literally.

He shared with me that he and his late wife found this house together and were excited to make it a home for them and their son Brandon. I was speechless but tried not to be. As a mother, I wanted to do everything in my power to help him as a single father. He was keeping his head up high through what I could only imagine would be the hardest, I mean hardest, time in his life. I was so hoping he would hire me for the job. Job offered, job accepted.

Mike and I are similar. We are picky; we need a lot of choices. Yet we are very decisive. When we find what we love we do not care the cost because we get so much joy out of it, the item is priceless.

I am not going to lie. I was very, VERY nervous on design day. I so badly wanted Mike to like what I was presenting. Mike and Brandon's home was part of a new construction neighborhood and unlike most of my meetings, I was setting up my large print outs, fabric, tile, wallpaper samples and everything else on a rather small rickety folding table in between the studs surrounding us. Sawdust was a-plenty and there was a lot of imagining to take place from a construction site to what would be the finished end product. Mike was happy, thank goodness!

Mike wanted a welcoming entryway that was impactful to guests visiting yet connected to him. We went bold with dark graphic wallpaper, a custom console and large art. My personal favorite is the artwork. I had the vintage Paris map I found on Etsy framed into four individual pieces. Paris is where Mike and his late wife fell in love. To me, design only has meaning if it is connected to the people that call the place their home. This was no exception.

the EVERYDAY

the BEAUTY

CUSTOM

One of the things I love about designing custom pieces is you get to determine the correct scale of the item for the room. In general, retail has some standard measurements for certain pieces. Console tables Are. The. Worst.

I know, it is a MAJOR first world problem.

It is however something that I run into a lot. Console tables are often way too short and too deep to fit most spaces we are trying to stuff them into. Why are they generally 30" high like a dining table where you are sitting? Kitchen counters hit you at 36". Seeing as I am irritated with the stubby and chubby console tables in the market, I prefer to design my own. Mainly because my job is to make sure the pieces I am suggesting fit and function in the space, but also because I get to work with local craftsman.

Welding, what an art. Any job you have to wear a mask for, I respect. Hockey goalies {for all my Canadian clients}, collecting honey, and welding. That is real work at its best folks.

For Mike's console I suggested stainless steel for the legs. The wood is one of my favorites; zebra. I have to give Mike props, shopping for wood with Brandon was hard. What parent wants to shop for anything, much less wood, with their young child? Aisle after aisle of walnut, cherry, birch, maple, cumaru and jatoba. No thank you. Brandon was awesome. It is just not what one wants to be doing as bonding experience with their child.

The end result is stunning as it pops off the wallpaper. It is unique and let me tell you the scale is magnificent!

house that love built

———

GREAT ROOM

the WANTS the WISHES

Mike's great room is GREAT. It has a massive vaulted ceiling with lots of tall windows. Vaulted ceilings are spectacular and I would take them any day over the standard 8' flat ceiling most homes have. They can however make the room feel cold if you do not add elements to bring the ceiling down allowing a more intimate space. This was a tricky one as the wall was so tall.

The fireplace was as basic as they come with 12"x12" beige tiles slapped on the drywall surrounding the gas fireplace. There was an empty alcove that needed a purpose. I was struggling with how to finish off these two elements and eventually came up with the idea to add a beam from corner to corner that gave the new tall fireplace surround and custom cabinet a stopping point.

Mike had expressed that he wanted a comfortable, casual family friendly room, easy to entertain in and yet still be formal at times. When he told me he actually throws a football together with Brandon in the room, I did not believe it at first. But then I saw it first hand and I realized at that moment I had helped turn the raw space we stood in on design day into a home.

the EVERYDAY

"We spend a lot of time relaxing and watching sports together in this space. I love that the room can be formal or informal so we can toss a football together."

the BEAUTY

truly tranquil

KITCHEN

FAMILY ROOM

DINING ROOM

PANTRY

CLOSET

OFFICE

LIVING ROOM

LAUNDRY

POWDER

CLOSET

ENTRY

UP

GARAGE

the HOUSE

sammamish, WA

built in 1999

2,900 SF

5 bed / 3 bath

traditional

the FAMILY

CHAD / engineer, physicist

TIFFANY / management consultant

KALEB / 7 years

TATE / 5 years

KODA / alaskan malamute

truly tranquil
_____

MASTER BATH

the WANTS the WISHES

One of my very first paid interior jobs was for Chad + Tiffany. I had little to no professional experience in interiors as I was transitioning from apparel design. Chad is best friend to my brother-in-law and put in a good word for me. The first few projects I worked on with them was for their previous home and they trusted my design expertise regardless of my experience in interiors. Soon they purchased a new home. Although they loved it overall, they did not love the master bath carpet. Whose idea was it to put carpet in bathrooms really?

That person should be fired, yesterday.

I get it, carpet is soft and warm under foot. But carpet around showers, tubs and other areas I do not need to mention makes me a bit nauseous. I cannot count the number of times we have ripped carpet out of bathrooms. Even when we are in the construction phase with only the subfloor it is by far a major improvement. The carpet was an easy design fix, next was the large corner jetted tub that almost every 1980's – 1990's home has. It is like the large elephant in the room collecting dust. They still desired a tub but they wanted it to take up less real estate and give a bit more space to the shower. Seeing as Chad is 6'6" we needed to give him a bit more elbow room. Why yes, I wore my tallest heels on design day and I still felt like a gymnast.

the EVERYDAY

Tile floors. A bit of an upgrade for sure. The downside? Cold, especially on gray chilly northwest days. For warmth underfoot we added heated floors and chose a porcelain tile with the appearance of wood to also warm it up visually.

Since we ripped out the dust collector and added a much smaller tub that really only Kaleb + Tate utilize, we had room for a small linen cabinet. The cabinet is highly functional and also adds more wood to the space. Bathrooms can tend to feel cold with all that tile laying around. In the end I am so grateful Chad + Tiffany trusted me yet again to help them with their home. When giving their friends and family a tour it has been said everyone tends to spend the most time admiring their bathroom.

Truly special clients, truly tranquil oasis.

the BEAUTY

east meets west

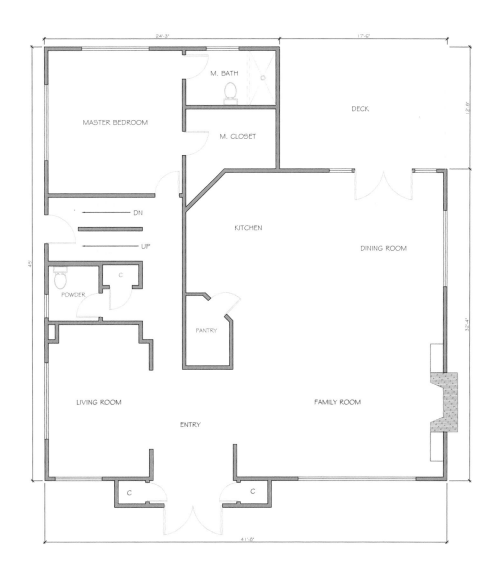

the HOUSE

kirkland, WA

built in 2014

4,600 SF

5 bed / 4.5 bath

transitional cape cod

the FAMILY

KEITH / president + executive

KATE / interior design project
manager

SAM / 4 years

MATT / 2 years

NORAH / lab mix
{she prefers purebred lab}

ELLA / cocker spaniel mix
{indifferent}

east meets west

———————————————————

ENTRY

the WANTS the WISHES

I am not sure if Kate actually had a verbal conversation with her husband Keith or more of a mental one to give me permission to design their entry. I am sure she sold it as a "benefit" of working for a small corporation of two. He was providing medical benefits for the family so this was her gift to him. Spouses have been known to be absent for Initial Consultations and Design Hand Off days which is never my preference. To truly do my job right I feel it is always important to hear what both parties like, do not like, where they want to splurge and where they want to be economical.

I am neutral. I am Switzerland.

I give the gift of bringing both of their design styles together regardless of how far apart they appear. Sometimes it is an effortless task, other times it is like cheering for the Patriots when under your breath you are routing for the Seahawks. Thankfully it was a Hawks day and off we went warming up their entry and adding some personality.

the EVERYDAY

Keith + Kate bought their home in a wonderful downtown Kirkland neighborhood. They were planning to remodel one bathroom but the project soon turned into demo down to the studs, entirely new floor plan and ultimately a custom built house almost doubling the square footage.

The great news is that their little bathroom remodel that evolved into a 4,600 SF house now has a bedroom for baby #3 on the way. Sometimes these things are meant to happen and this was no exception.

Matt + Sam often take over most of the space in the entry as they can hear the adults prepping dinner in ear shot and can spread out their ever growing train track. Norah + Ella make sure the entry rug is always warm for guests.

Since their home does not have a garage, this is the main entry that functions for the day to day. One of the elements I wanted in the space was a sentimental piece that has meaning to them both. We hired a local artist to create something custom that brings Keith's east coast closer to her west coast. Funny story: Kate did not want to have kids and she especially did not want to get married. Then she met Keith. Keith proposed, Kate accepted and by Christmas 2016 they will be a family of five. I love that the art represents his hometown of Manchester and her origin in Seattle coming together and uniting.

the BEAUTY

CUSTOM

I love this custom art and frame. I have a small obsession with maps. This one is extra special as it has meaning to the clients. It makes a statement when guests walk into the entry and adds a pop of color. I designed the art to be two pieces and the frame to be two identical frames connected as one. The metal welded city names adds dimension to the art and I love the way Keith's hometown of Manchester ends on his new home here on the west coast. We are happy to have you Keith!

dudes dwelling

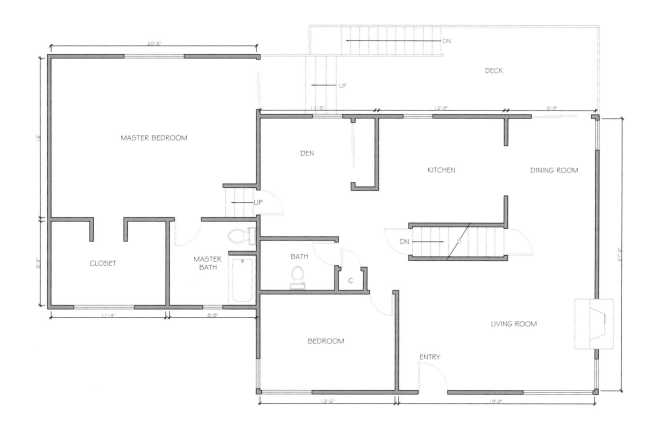

the HOUSE

bellevue, WA

built in 1942

3,000 SF

3 bed / 3 bath

traditional

the FAMILY

MIKE / angel investor

JAKE / 16 years {not shown}

+ visiting neighbor girls

JIMMY / mini schnauzer

dudes dwelling

DINING ROOM

the WANTS the WISHES

Mike bought this house because it was blocks from Jake's mother's home. Location, great. House, needed a lot of love. It was a flip, and truth be told, there are great flips and there are flops with things like cultured stone slapped on the drywall surrounding the fireplace with no attention to detail. Mike's was the latter.

I will take an older home over a new construction tract home any day of the week. The main reason is that older homes have more of a story, more quirks and defiantly more challenges. It not only makes my job much more interesting it also means I am forever learning which I love.

Mike's dining room was very narrow. I guess you could call it a dining room but really it was more like a hallway. Light? Optional. Function? None. Unless you count hitting your head on the dangling chandelier shortly after bumping your hip on the door leading upstairs. Solutions? Always. I can hardly sleep after an Initial Consultation where there are problems that need to be solved. Thankfully Mike let me do my thing and trusted all that I proposed. He handed over the keys so I could start taking down walls, adding the new pair of massive French doors, three adorable windows and removed the want-to-be-stone fireplace.

the EVERYDAY

In order to allow the dining room to serve as a functioning room I had to shift everything to one wall to create usable space. We needed room to walk through into the kitchen and to the deck. We also gained a lot of seating by adding a custom built-in bench. Delivered pizza (one of Mike's specialties) is much more delicious when lounging VS dining for sure.

Challenges are exhilarating. They also are very, very challenging. Asbestos? Thank goodness the test came back negative, lord knows a hazmat suit is not as flattering as my normal get up. Knob + tube wiring? Yes and yes. Plumbing so old we had to replace it throughout the home. Unfortunately yes for everyone especially Mike's pocketbook. Did I mention the location of the neighborhood is to die for?

When the plaster finally settled, the paint was dry and the fire was ripping I still look forward to hearing from Mike. He is one of those people who is really living life, not just living.

I only wish he would buy another flip (or flop).

the BEAUTY

RECLAIMED

This may be my favorite custom piece to date. I adore reclaiming solid wood and bringing it back to life. My favorite wood guy, Steve has a home "shop" (really it's his garage and most of his backyard) where I wish I could frequent more often as he has so much to choose from. It is just a matter of finding the right dimensions and species. Speaking of species, Steve knows everything, I mean everything about all types of wood, the origin, the history and everything in-between. When he starts talking it is as if he is telling a story. He is so passionate it is hard not to follow suit. I was in luck because I went there to source a variety of wood for Mike's custom, one-of-a-kind table. I walked away with maple, walnut, cumaru, zebra, jatoba, birch and hickory. The woodworker and welder executed my design perfectly and I only wish they would make one for me!

Rumor has it a kitchen remodel takes a

weekend.

DESIGN. Like a fine wine.

DESIGN, people want it yesterday.
The thing about design is it takes time.

Like with most things creative, it is a process and time is the active ingredient. I once had a roofer suggest a foolproof strategy to make my job easier. He said, you should create three designs and offer them to all of your clients. Dear client, here is design 1, design 2, and design 3. Now pick from the plethora of choices and it will become your dream home. It took me a minute to not laugh hysterically. Does this dude know anything about design? No, he runs a successful roofing company. I can't keep a house dry as a bone and shelter those who reside in it, why would he know how to do my job? Design to me is so, so much more than a choice.

It is your voice.
It is your story.

Designs come to me while I am processing them, when I am thinking about how to do something different. How to make the design unique and meaningful to the people living there. I see something, hear something and it triggers an idea. Kate's EAST MEETS WEST entry is a perfect example. When Kate and I talked about having me help her with their entry I was excited. It was grand. It had opportunity. What it was missing was a story. One night when I was cleaning up from dinner it came to me. Kate had often talked about how she never saw herself having children and for sure was never getting married.

In walks Keith.
Months later they were eating cake.
Then Sam.
Then Matt.
Then baby boy #3 on the way.

Keith, an east coast Patriots loving fan, met Kate, a Seattle native and he changed her story. They came from two faraway lands and found a common ground because love conquers all. While scrubbing the last pot I could see it. Two coastlines far away, yet connected. Not at first glance, that was the point. I had to flush out the design concept and work with the artist. The last thing I wanted was to have the middle of a map chopped out which would look very odd. Thankfully the artist had the brilliant idea of flipping the coastlines, making the art abstract at first glance and in turn, making Manchester and Seattle closer. I like telling stories, but I love the stories that whisper. Keith a successful business professional dealing with numbers, distribution, and manufacturing, did not get it. I was not surprised. He is like most of my clients, they do not fully understand the design but they say go for it, they trust, and they love it.

Manchester woos Seattle. It is the two of them. It is their story.

I hear it often, "I keep picking the same

NUDGE. Just enough to keep my day job.

NUDGE, just a bit. You meet the clients, understand their wants + wishes, their styles and then you want to push them outside their comfort zone.

Just a skosh.

I hear it often, "I keep picking the same colors. I guess because I am comfortable with them, but I really want something different." So I nudge just enough to make sure the design does not look like their past homes, or every other house on the block.

blue."

Now if a client says I want blue and green, I need to stick to that. If I show up on design day and have a color palette of orange and red, they would fire me on the spot. If they say they hate white painted cabinets and only want stained cabinets, it is important to abide by that. My goal is not to persuade them or not allow them to be who they are. It is to keep within the parameters they are outlining and nudge just beyond.

Believe me there are a lot of days where I am picking out yet another shade of blue {who does not love blue?}. Virtually every one of my past, present and future clients loves some shade of blue.

A shaker cabinet door.
A white subway tile.

With one of my most loyal clients Amy, this process of nudging comes up at every design hand off day. Amy and her husband Jeff have allowed me to design one room at a time for them over a four year period. Amy often has the same response to at least one item I have presented on design day. "A DAYBED?!!! Whoa, I am not sure how I feel about a daybed." I encourage clients to process and sleep on the designs before making any final decisions, as they are personal and expensive choices. About a week later Amy and I checked in and she said she was warming up to the idea but was still a little skeptical. In the end she allowed me to nudge her just a bit. Guess what turned out to be her favorite piece in the room?

You are correct. The daybed.

Every client who has allowed me to nudge, even if they are unsure in the beginning of the design process, are thrilled with the end result.

Are you kidding me? It arrived in the wrong

BROKEN. Oh too often.

BROKEN, like how broken? A scratch or shattered? We waited 6 weeks for this tub and it is broken?

I used to say 1 in 10 products we work with shows up broken, scratched, damaged, the wrong color, size, pattern, print, sheen or finish. Products are often discontinued {after ordering and paying in full} or they are backordered for a months. "Wait, now it is going to be six weeks, maybe seven? Does that include the shipping time? No, that is just how long it is backordered. It will take an additional two weeks for shipping as long as there is not another snow storm back east, then it may take three."

These days it feels more like 1 in 6.

It is not surprising really. When we are working on full room designs, remodels and multiple rooms at once, we manage a LOT of products. All retailers and vendors have fulfillment issues or defective products. Really, it is just life. The challenge is that when one item has a problem, it almost always affects the entire project.

Kitchen counters arrived in the wrong finish.
We approved satin, they arrived polished.

HALT!

Counters cannot go in.
Call countertop fabricator, find out issue, solve issue, and get new date for install.
Cross your fingers they have satin in stock. And 2 full slabs.
Backsplash cannot go in, call tile installer, reschedule so he will not show up on the clients' doorstep at 8AM with trowel in hand.
Call electrician, plumber, and painter. Reschedule all of them.
Call client, explain the situation that is completely out of your control.
Job on hold for 10 days waiting for correct counters.
Client not happy.
Calm down client.

It is the process we try hard to explain. This happens at EVERY job to EVERY person. There are so many products, materials and details. Each one affects the other. I wish it were not the case but it just is. Our job is to pick up the broken pieces and create solutions and keep everyone as pleasant as possible through the chaos of remodeling.

Now who has the Advil and Mac & Jack's?

finish?

I can do a lot of things short of being a

TIMELESS. I wish I had that superpower.

"TIMELESS, that is what I want my design to be," says the client. I do not disagree. I just do not think I have that kind of power. Design has to change or nothing will ever sell. If things do not look outdated there is never a reason to update, upgrade or reinvent. What would all those stores do with all those timeless products just sitting looking pretty on the shelves? I am a fan of evolving and being as timeless as possible without being basic and predictable.

I do not follow trends that are the here and now, the today. Trends get you to buy the newest items of the moment, it is the American way. I love new, creative ideas, solutions and materials that keep design interesting and fresh but to me there is a big difference. Fashion is a four season business. I am fine with buying the new silhouette of jeans every year, but I certainly do not want to remodel my kitchen every couple of years.

magician.

Funny story. Julie is our drapery specialist. She has made most of the custom drapes, pillows and cushions in this book. She asked me to design her kitchen and requested a timeless design. I get it, kitchens are the heart of the home and above all, expensive.

Very expensive.

But how can you make something timeless in a forever changing industry? The reason the industry changes is to make the things you bought a few years ago look old so you will buy more stuff from them.

And at a higher price.

Julie does her research. She is the ideal client in the sense that she knows where to splurge and where to save, she trusts the design perspective and sees the value in it. After she took some time to do her research we met and she said, "You are right, all of the kitchen design books from ten years ago look dated." So we set out to make the most timeless design possible while drastically updating the function and layout.

Design. Hardly timeless. Forever changing.

To say I wear many hats is an under-

SAVING LIVES. One paint chip at a time.

SAVING LIVES, not a part of the job description. My children's father is a firefighter. I have loads of friends who are social workers. My sisters are each raising three children all while having side gigs.

I am a designer. I shop for a living. I make things look pretty.
Look perfect.

At a glance, that may be what the job is, or appears to be from the outside and rightfully so. But I believe we ARE making a difference in people's lives. We help give our clients a space they truly want to be in, where they connect with their family and make meaningful memories.

We do so much more than pick out the right color for the wall or make sure the drapes are hung at the right height. We help when spouses are not seeing eye-to-eye. We help find a solution where both are completely represented without compromising the overall design. We sit dead center between our trusting clients and our loyal partners and trades.

We are the bridge.

We calm down a client when their countertop arrives in the wrong material, then hang up, call the countertop fabricator to fix the problem, and fix it yesterday while still using our nice voice. All relationships are equally valuable, and crucial, to the success of our business.

15%	Designer.
25%	Marital Counselor {schooling not necessary}.
45%	Babysitter of all details, products, materials, house keys, and people needed at the job site at. Any. Given. Moment.
30%	Diplomat.
15%	Emails, text messages at 6:20am, phone calls and last minute face to face meeting with clients, trades or really just anyone.

Yes, that is more than 100 percent but I did state simple math was not my strength and remodeling is extremely tricky. If only we knew what was behind every wall, below every floor joist, if products arrived unbroken, damaged, in the right color, finish, sheen, size all while arriving on time with no shipping delays, nobody ever got hurt, sick or had a family emergency. Our job would be a whole hell of lot easier.

That is not reality.

For us, our goal is to keep everyone forward moving. We know that in the end if we create solutions to the ever growing challenges we face, we will reach the finish line with happy clients, partners and trades with a glass of bubbly in hand. There is a reason our email signatures sign off with cheers, we have to keep the end goal in mind, always.

statement.

raise the roof

featured on HGTV 425 Gray houzz

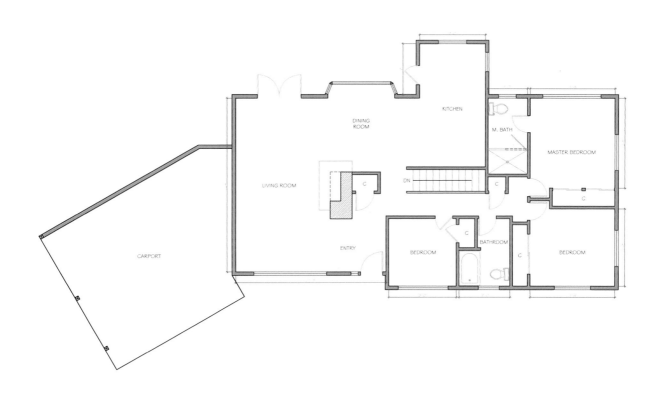

the HOUSE

kirkland, WA

built in 1963

2,900 SF

5 bed / 3 bath

mid century modern

the FAMILY

HARMONY / interior designer

HOLDEN / 4 years

EMMA / 1 year

raise the roof

———————

KITCHEN

the WANTS the WISHES

   This by far is my most sentimental design to date, the one I am most proud of and the design that was first to be featured in a magazine. I am still in awe that even though I am self-taught in interior design this room was 1 of 11 finalists in the HGTV's Fresh Faces of Design national competition of 2015.

   It is also the hardest to write about.

   This is my family house where I brought both of my babies home. Where Holden and Emma's father and I remodeled one room at a time turning the ugly, sometimes smelly 1960's original into our home. I spent endless hours dreaming up the ever-evolving kitchen design in my head and many, many floor plan changes. Ultimately we decided to add on to the square footage and raise the roof that was under the average 8'. We bumped it up to 10' with a new gable, exposed beam and four large skylights.

   I love to cook. Love to entertain. To date I had never had a new kitchen. This was literally a dream come true after years of seeing my clients faces light up when they get to walk into their new space and fire up a pan. When designing for my clients I have to be a bit conservative and abide by their wants + wishes. Designing for yourself is where you can take the most risks and be bold in your choices. I had become bored with the predictable "window over the sink, upper cabinets on either side" layout you see in almost every home. I wanted something more interesting, less expected. I also wanted a ton of light. We have so many gray, overcast days you can never have too much natural light. So I designed the space to have a large 4'x6' window surrounded by textured natural slate to focus on the beautiful green trees all the Pacific Northwest rain gives us.

   My client was very happy with the end result.

the EVERYDAY

"There is not a moment where Emma isn't on my hip while I'm making my morning latté. It would not be the same without her assistance and smile to wake me up."

I always desired an island but even with the newly added square footage we did not have the space. I rearranged the peninsula to make it feel like an island and created highly functional zones so we were not bumping into each other and guests had a place to hang. My favorite zone is the espresso corner where you can work independently from the chef making breakfast while enjoying the view outside.

I love marble countertops. I do however love red wine.

In the end, quartzite stone was the winner. It looks a bit like marble, is stronger than granite and much more resistant to staining. It is the perfect material to roll out dough and make memories.

Cooking with my kids brings me joy and a time where we focus on creating something together. Holden loves his mini rolling pin I picked up at an antique store and uses it when we make our homemade pizza dough. Emma is never far behind and quickly knows it is time to find the step stool. Seeing the two of them hard at work, being creative together makes my heart melt.

That is the dream come true, not the house, not the kitchen.

the BEAUTY

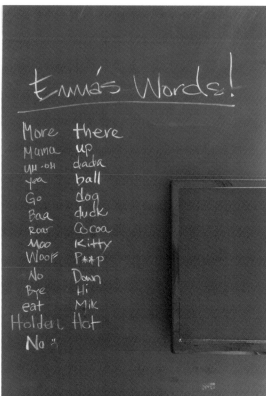

RECLAIMED

I love, love, love bold contrast. I also do not love the look of a TV on the wall, as it is a black rectangle when not in use that is a bit unsightly. We decided to add a small TV in the kitchen as we only had a television in the basement. I wanted it to visually go away as much as possible and stumbled across reclaimed slate stone that was originally in a UPS office. I quickly called my fabricator {this is an upgrade from chalk paint, it is the real deal} and he fabricated the slate into three panels. I adore natural materials and all things repurposed. I knew I needed something old for all of the new in my kitchen and this was a perfect solution.

CUSTOM

There was not room for a walk in pantry in my kitchen. I am not a fan of a small reach-in pantry with drywall walls and a swing door as I feel you loose a lot of space. The 4"+ walls on either side and the swing of the door takes up a lot of room. I wanted to utilize every inch of space we had so I came up with a unique design that has been a favorite on HOUZZ (110K saves, what?!!!) and a favorite of my kids. I designed shallow drawers at their height and loaded it with snacks for them. The other drawers work perfectly for items that are hard to stack like bags of beans, pasta, potatoes and onions. Function is a must for me as I like things organized and to have a place. It defiantly turned out better than I anticipated.

home away from home

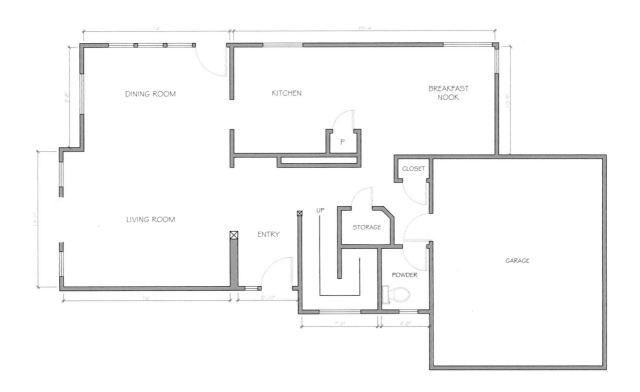

the HOUSE

redmond, WA

built in 1995

1,950 SF

3 bed / 2.5 bath

traditional

the FAMILY

HAMISH / VP international business development

STEPHANIE / winery sales + marketing director

BLAIR / 23 years + off to college

HAMILTON / lhasa apso

TUX / lab, whippet mix

home away from home

MASTER BATH

the WANTS the WISHES

Hamish and I worked together at a local running apparel and footwear company a decade ago before I had shifted into interiors. Without his trust in my {lack of} expertise in interior design I would not have had the opportunity to transition from apparel design. He not only allowed me to design his entire home {prior to meeting, falling in love and marrying his bride Stephanie}, he needed me to manage the entire remodel as he is often jetting off abroad to do his job. Throughout the process I built strong relationships with everyone necessary to do the work. It allowed me the freedom to not only design but to execute the designs to the end product and manage. Every. Single. Detail.

Blessing? Yes. Curse. Some days it felt like it.

But I worked through it. I learned hundreds of things that brings me to today where Kate and I have a full service design and remodel firm. I am so grateful for Hamish, his trust and the freedom he gave me to learn.

Stephanie is co-founder of a local Washington winery and was one day pouring Hamish a glass of red. They hit it off and were soon walking down the aisle. Seeing as Hamish works in International business it was only fitting that he accepted a job abroad shortly after we finished his remodel. They currently call Amsterdam home and my portfolio their second home.

The great news for me was that the bathroom had zero personality. We gutted everything and started fresh. The empty corner below the windows had no purpose. By adding a vanity counter connected to the main cabinet in the empty corner, it now has a function and looks purposeful. The large graphic wallpaper with the mosaic marble backsplash gives plenty of interest while still allowing the space to feel calm.

the BEAUTY

home away from home

OFFICE + LAUNDRY

the WANTS the WISHES

This was a fun one. The upstairs had two bedrooms and an open area large enough to be a third bedroom with a reach in closet that housed the washer and dryer. We reworked the floor plan in order to create a true third bedroom and moved the W/D to one of the new large office closets. They needed the room to function for laundry but wanted it hidden. At the time of design it was just Hamish living here so he needed a desk to work in the evenings. We have problems all the time with products arriving broken, damaged and in the wrong color, finish, or you name it.

For once this worked to our advantage. Hamish's desk arrived with a couple of deep scrapes in the wood. After sitting on hold with the manufacturer for for what felt like an hour they decided to send us a new one and requested we keep the damaged one. In the end it was meant to be. Better than my original design, the two desks facing each other now functions to fold laundry and Stephanie has a place to call her own when marketing her Merlot.

Accidents can sometimes be happy. In this case very happy.

the EVERYDAY

"We work a lot and travel a lot but rarely do we take ourselves too seriously!"

the BEAUTY

country culinary

featured on **houzz**

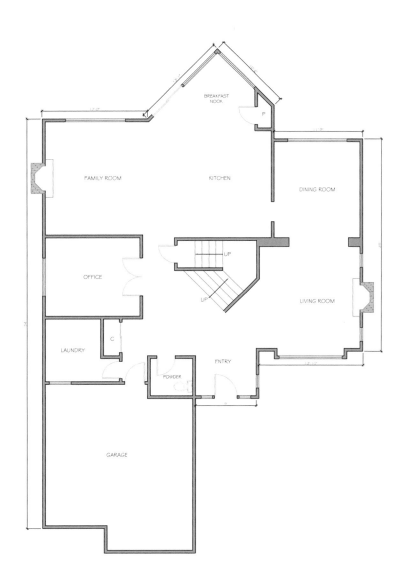

the HOUSE

maltby, WA

built in 1994

2,800 SF

4 bed / 2.5 bath

traditional

the FAMILY

BEDE / aerospace service engineer

JULIE / drapery specialist + manufacturer

MATT / 16 years

CURT / 22 years + off to college

CHEECH + CHEDDAR

country culinary

KITCHEN

the WANTS the WISHES

Julie is not only a client but, one of my favorite people to work with because she makes my job easier. She always follows through and specializes in the details. She is our drapery specialist and has manufactured all of our clients' custom drapes and everything else in between. When she asked me to help her with her kitchen after she had picked out her backsplash and counters, I was happy to help her bring it all together.

This was by far one of my hardest projects to wrap my head around in regards to design aesthetic. I have my own style but I try very hard never to push my personal taste onto any of my clients.

I want their homes to look like them. Not me.

The reason it was extremely hard was because I have a handful of design rules I live and die by. Regardless of my clients design style, I tend to preach the same general rules as I feel very strongly about them. One rule is having a variation of color and tone of floors to cabinets so it all doesn't blend together and feel overwhelming. For Julie + Bede's kitchen they knew they defiantly wanted to keep their oak floors the natural color and not add stain. This I agreed with wholeheartedly as why make oak look like walnut, or espresso beans? Let the wood be the species of wood it is instead of giving it a costume or dressing it up as if it needed a makeover.

the EVERYDAY

Where I struggled was with wood floors with wood cabinets in similar tones. Although we chose a cherry for the cabinets that had a bit of a gray undertone in the stain, it still felt like a lot of wood to me. However, what is important is that the clients are happy as they are writing the checks and living there. In the end I nudged Julie and Bede a tad and they went with my idea of adding white upper cabinets to the cook top wall and for the nook bench.

Bede is the culinary specialist of the family, he spends hours behind his BBQ, so having a functional kitchen beyond a doubt was key. Their current kitchen had an odd shaped island that was not all that functional. It also was too close to the family room sofa and the breakfast nook making the whole space feel cramped. The space in the middle of the 90's shaped island seemed big enough to square dance in. Reworking the island took some nudging but in the end they trusted my vision.

Their family gathers here daily to reconnect with each other. It is a fantastic multi-tasking space. Typically one person is actively cooking and others are nearby talking about what happened that day. Bede watches cooking shows and cooks to relax while Julie reads the morning paper.

the BEAUTY

salvaged for perspective

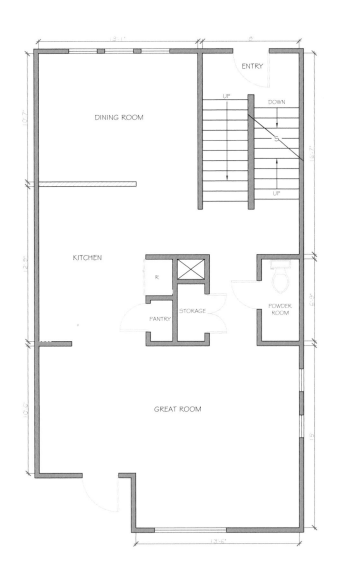

the HOUSE

bothell, WA

built in 2008

1,950 SF

3 bed + office / 4 bath

transitional

the FAMILY

ADAM / software engineer

MEGAN / homemaker + aspiring
novelist

BEN / 10 years

NATE / 8 years

salvaged for perspective

GREAT ROOM

the WANTS the WISHES

This was a tall order. At some point after hearing what was needed in Adam + Megan's newly downsized home I was thinking I had been hired to be a magician, not a designer. I met Megan for the first time in their large Kirkland home they had just sold in order to move into a much smaller house in the nearby downtown Bothell neighborhood. I got the down low of their wants + wishes for their new great room as the room had a tall order.

A space to read, and play games together as a family.
Seating for entertaining small and large gatherings with family + friends.
A place to house, play with and tuck away their ever growing LEGO collection.
Additional storage for all other toys not stamped with LEGO.
New flooring that was hard enough to withstand Adam's hobby of rhythm skating yet still be cozy and comfortable when not rolling.
Be able to pull out large floor matts for Megan's ballet practice.
Oh yes. And a piano.

Seeing as there was not a lot of square footage {don't be fooled by the wide-angle lens} we ripped out the large electric fireplace and wall-to-wall drywall bookshelf. Thank goodness as it was not doing anybody any favors. Carpet, gone and replaced with hickory hardwoods and a large area rug that could be rolled up for Adam. Thankfully they room had 9' ceilings so we used that to our advantage and added custom built-in cabinets in a corner that had no purpose prior. We lightened up the paint, added additional lighting and somehow found a spot for the ebony and ivory.

the EVERYDAY

As a family they chose to downsize in order to obtain a less hectic life so Adam could commute to work on two wheels VS four along the Burke Gillman Trail. They loved the fact that they could now walk to local spots and would be closer to the boys' school as traffic over the last few years feels like it doubled. They desired less time in the car and more time together as a family so they sacrificed square footage for location.

The benefits were plenty. The challenge was being in a downtown neighborhood they were much closer to their neighbors and had a front row seat of the backyard hobbies and deflated swimming pools. We needed a solution to salvage the light but not focus on the things we did not want to see outside. Adam + Megan are such fun clients to work for as they trusted all I threw at them. I soon sourced some vintage windows to give just enough of a blurred perspective, keeping the light coming in while adding charm.

the BEAUTY

RECLAIMED

Hunting in one of my favorite architectural salvage yards, I found this pair of vintage windows I knew would be perfect to disguise the view of the neighbors' very close backyard, while still allowing light in. They not only block the view but they add so much character to the room and are often a conversation starter. I absolutely love giving something old a new purpose and bring it back to life!

CUSTOM

When designing this massive custom LEGO cabinet for my clients, we wanted the kids to be able to access and play in the space, yet be able to tuck away when not in use. I did not want a wall of all cabinets; I wanted it to feel warmer so I added a little nook in the middle to invite people in. The pull out trays function as desks and the tuck away doors work great for the day to day.

salvaged for perspective

OFFICE

the WANTS the WISHES

After completing most of the main floor Megan asked if I could take a look at the office on the ground floor. It was next to the garage and the only other room on that floor was a bathroom. They had no idea what to do with it and there was more furniture than square footage in the space. All I saw was potential.

Since the family downsized and they have their great room, dining room and kitchen on the main floor that is heavily used by all, this space was a gold mine. It was an opportunity to give the family an away room, a space to be alone and enjoy some peace and quiet a floor below. They wanted to read, write and hang out in a place that was comfortable and welcoming. Megan needed an area to retreat to so she could focus on her writing. It has become a perfect place for them to curl up on the couch and have a long telephone conversation without being disturbed.

Artwork is one of those things that is very personal and I find it difficult to suggest for people as it is so subjective. After hearing about all of Nate's + Ben's artwork I thought it was the perfect opportunity to honor them and yet make the room feel a bit more whimsical. We loaded the main wall with the boys' art which naturally gave us an unlimited color palette. Megan was not scared of prints so I jumped at the chance to suggest a fun fabric for the sofa as lord knows I have picked out a few tan, beige, grey, and taupe sofas. I sourced reclaimed purple heart wood from my favorite reclaimed wood shop in Kirkland for the floating bookshelf. I had been dying to use purple heart for years. Who knew there is wood that is actually purple? This was the space! Since there was an HVAC soffit in the room I wanted the new shelf to tie into it so it would not look so out of place.

Truth be told before the redesign, the room felt utilitarian, crowded and they never used it. Now they use the room every day and it feels like a calm sanctuary.

the EVERYDAY

"Ben often escapes to the office to enjoy some uninterrupted time. Once Nate notices Ben's absence, he joins him quickly changing the dynamics of the room."

RECLAIMED

Steve my favorite reclaimed wood supplier had been showing me purple heart for years. I knew there would come a day where I could use it for a project and today was the day. We had already picked out a graphic purple and gray sofa fabric so it was just the thing to finish out the desk area. A corner to corner floating shelf gives their books a place to rest while not being too serious and adding some of nature's purple.

May 8th, 2015
Dear Mom,
I appreciate you for helping me with everything and treating me with respect. I also enjoy Spending time with you. My favorite thing to do with you is sit in the sun.
I gave you this art because I think you will like this very much. I wish you a Happy Mothers Day!
Love,
Ben

CUSTOM

The custom bulletin board in a beautiful textured fabric and white frame is one-of-a-kind. I designed it to be a bit oversized so there was a lot of room to display all of their sentimental pieces. When I was taking the family's "everyday" photos for this book, I could not help but notice the heartwarming letter from Ben to his mom for Mother's Day. Clearly the bulletin board has been put to good use and I was delighted.

reclaimed space

featured on HGTV houzz

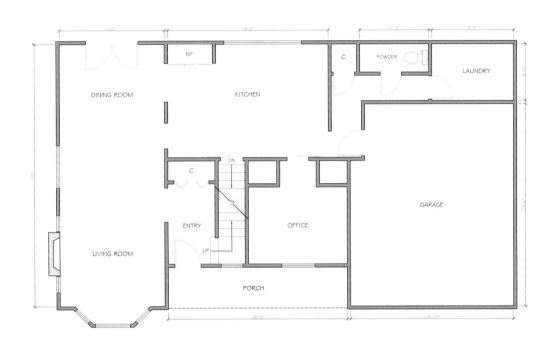

the HOUSE

kenmore, WA

built in 2001

2,900 SF

4 bed / 3.5 bath

transitional

the FAMILY

DARRYL / VP, systems + technology

TAMBIE / web developer + project
manager

ROCKET + DUKE
retired racing greyhounds,
although they occasionally
enjoy a quick sprint

reclaimed space

KITCHEN

the WANTS the WISHES

Tambie was referred to me through Amy {technically serine} as they work together at a little software company in Redmond. I have a dry sense of humor and can usually spot my like-minded right off the bat.

Darryl threw me for a loop though as he is DRY.

I try to be professional, yet personal at the same time. He kept me on my toes. I quickly discovered Darryl is agreeable and go with the flow until there is something he feels very strongly about.

Cue dry sense of humor.

Thank goodness we speak the same language or I think I would have walked away after our meeting with a slight misunderstanding of his wants + wishes.

Thankfully Darryl + Tambie both love greens and I got a much needed break from my old friend, the color blue. Almost everyone loves blue so I get a lot of requests to find the perfect B.L.U.E. for everyone's home. Blue is my California roll. I can imagine the look on my favorite sushi chef's face when my 4 year old orders yet another California roll that he has made a half of a million times. He is 4 and eats sushi, so let's give him a hall pass.

Green. And so I was off, searching for the perfect green elements to bring into the space. I wanted to compliment the newly added 9' long window we popped in front of the sink gazing at the evergreen cedars outside.

the EVERYDAY

We could not raise the 8' ceiling because there is a floor above. We did not want to bump out and add on as that would be too costly.

Then it came to me.

Hallways. Necessary, yet a lot of space for really just one activity; walking.

I knew if we could take out the wall that separated the kitchen from the hallway we would not only gain a lot of space but we would lighten up the entire floor. I just had to solve the hallway factor through design. The last thing I wanted was the kitchen to feel like it was smack dab in the middle of a hallway. There was a reach in hallway closet with a bi-fold door {do not even get me started} we were able to utilize the space for a new cabinet pantry. We stole a bit space from the entry coat closet for a coffee station and had ribbon mahogany sliding doors made. One door leading to the office, the other to the floor below. By replacing the hallway closet with a floor to ceiling pantry and a similar look for the coffee station, they now along with the new doors felt apart of the new space.

Tambie often works on the new island or enjoys a cup of tea with her mom as they catch up on their day. I still cannot believe the edge of the island was where the hallway was and how much real estate and light we gained.

Darryl is the chef of the house while Tambie does a mean mise en place and aspires to someday graduate to sous chef. Tambie is one of the sweetest people I know, she even crochet a blanket for my new daughter Emma. Deserving of a big celebration for a milestone birthday, Darryl decided to take the night off. He hired Tilth, a local organic restaurant and let them take over the kitchen to cook for her closest friends and family. What a celebration!

I am happy to hear that the kitchen not only functions for Darryl to whip up something on a daily basis, but it also worked for professional chefs, and many of them at once. Elated with the overall design, additional space, lots of new light and a very; very functional kitchen we achieved for Duke + Rocket.

the Beau

CUSTOM

The new island was ultra long, which we all loved. I was also worried it may feel overwhelming all in one counter material. I did not want the island to feel like a bowling lane by any means. We had a 3" thick walnut butcher block made for the end of the island which creates a great workspace to chop away directly across from the range. I love the way it warms up the space and breaks up the island.

technically serene

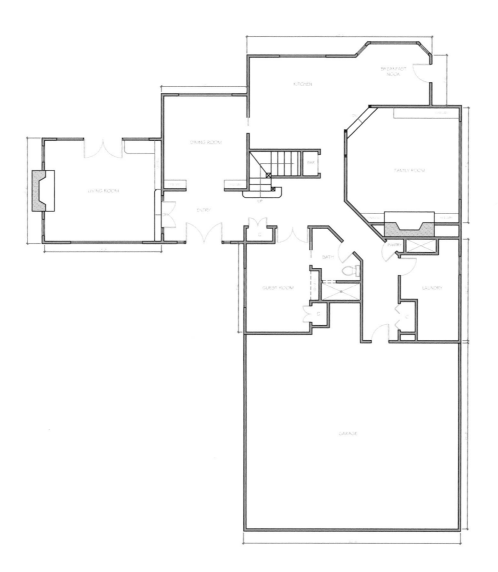

the HOUSE

mercer island, WA

built in 1987

3,400 SF

4 bed / 3 bath

traditional

the FAMILY

JEFF / software engineer

AMY / search analyst

LYLA / 7 years

CASSIE / 4 years

FRITZ + SNICKERS

technically serene

ENTRY

the WANTS the WISHES

Loyal. That is what Jeff + Amy are. They not only ask me back over and over to make a bunch of noise, dust and give them a finished room but they always make me feel at home. I think Amy has made me a latte more times than my local coffee shop.

Then came the entry and stairway project.

I was worried the lattes would stop. Worst yet I would not be asked back.

You think a kitchen remodel is invasive? Try a stairway. It literally affects every room in the house as it is the bridge. The bridge under construction. As Amy put it, the project was painful, but in the end totally worth it.

This was the 5th space I had designed and executed for Jeff + Amy and it was by far the most challenging for loads of reasons I will not bore you with. Cassie may have stopped napping all together during this process, which as a mama I know is devastating. Those hours when your little one is sleeping are precious.

the EVERYDAY

Carpet on the stairs was replaced with black stained oak treads and white risers. 1980's called and asked for their oak railing and spindles back.

We obliged.

Now the wall. The massively tall stairway wall that was staring at me, as were Jeff + Amy. Both were begging for a solution to dress up the drywall. I was stumped. There is wainscoting throughout most of their main floor and it would look dwarfed against the tall ceilings, plus too predictable. This is where design takes time. Thankfully they were patient with me and I eventually came up with a solution. We had MDF panels hand cut to two sizes, installed floor to ceiling and painted white. I love the end result, as it is not bold or drastic, it just adds interest. The black and white is timeless and hopefully they will not be getting a call in the future for this railing.

The new bench functions for putting shoes on and bags packed as they head out for their day. We added a collection of custom antiqued picture frames with snapshots of their life and family to tie in the hallway. Thankfully, months later I got an email from Amy. She asked if I had time to help them with their formal living room.

I can smell the espresso already.

the BEAUTY

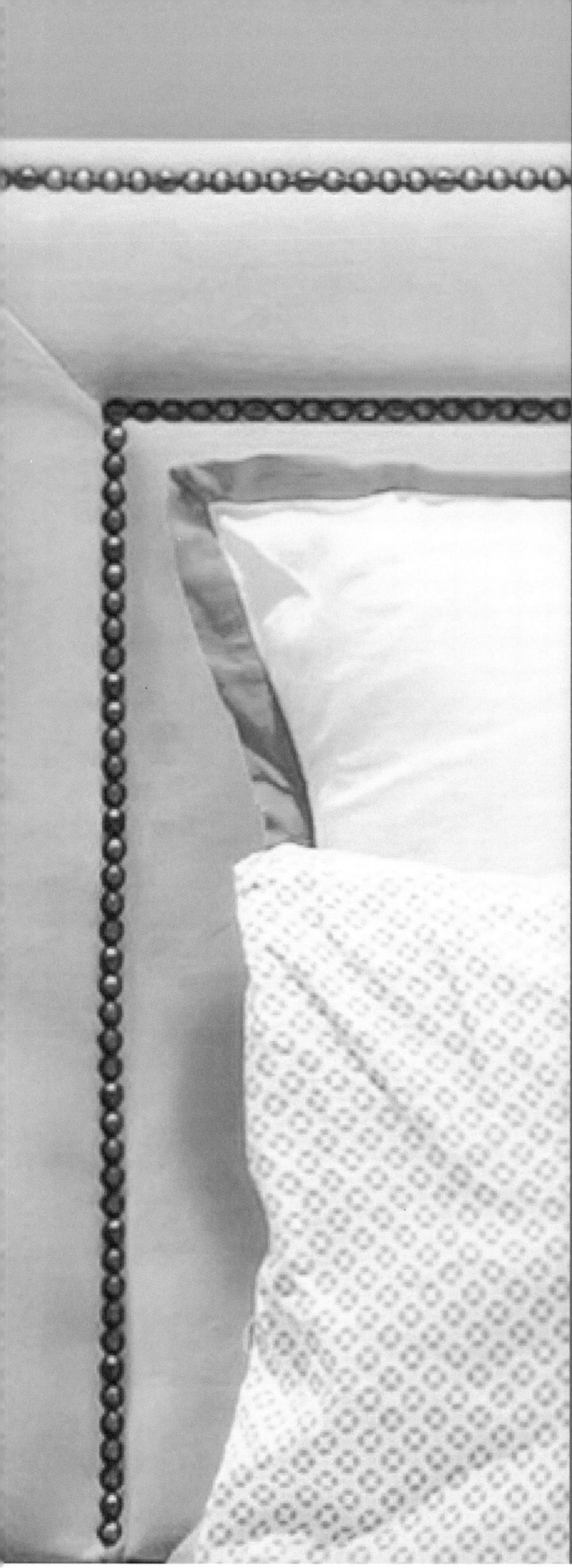

technically serene

GUEST ROOM

the WANTS the WISHES

This was a small project. We kept about half of the pieces they already had in their guest room. I had to showcase the room, not because of the design, but because of the meaning the space has to their family. Even though it is a guest room, the quarters get frequent use as Amy's dad; Lyla + Cassie's Pop Pop spends two nights a week at their home caring for the girls every need while Jeff + Amy head off to work. Seeing as Amy's parents live on Vashon Island which is a drive, ferry boat and another drive to Mercer Island, it only makes sense to stay over.

Pop Pop gets to be involved in the day to day with everyone yet he has his own separate space from the rest of the house. They love that the guest bedroom and bathroom are on the first floor, away from the main bedrooms upstairs. The room feels detached but still a part of the house since it is just a few steps from the kitchen and family room.

To say their family is close is an understatement. I have had the pleasure of witnessing it first hand, which melts my heart.

the EVERYDAY

The Pacific Northwest

FLAVORS

MICHAEL CHIARELLO'S CASUAL COOKING

COOK with JAMIE
JAMIE OLIVER

technically serene

DINING ROOM

the WANTS the WISHES

The dining room was the first room I designed for Jeff + Amy. The blue carpet and original dated chandelier were not cutting it. It is not a room they use everyday but it is the first room you see when you enter into their home. They wanted to add some personality, make a statement, and the room to feel a tad formal. They have a casual nook off the kitchen they use for most family meals so they wanted this to be special.

The wainscoting is original to the home, but it was aged oak which very much dated it. Prior to hiring me they had made some overall design changes and painted all of wainscoting, millwork white. Thank goodness. The floor to ceiling windows are to die for, along with the lake view and their enormous Japanese maple.

the EVERYS

"We love having special gatherings in this space
creating fond memories together."

There was not a lot of space in the room for storage or countertops to hold dishes, food and drinks. I proposed floor to ceiling custom cabinets that frame the large walkthrough to the entry. This allowed enough space to have a functional piece when they entertain while allowing lots of seating and kept the walkway to the kitchen free. Adding wallpaper in the back of the upper cabinet adds a bit of whimsy to their formal room.

Banquettes. A personal favorite as they serve a dual purpose. If you want to snuggle up to the person next to you it is a win-win. At a holiday family dinner if there are a few people not getting along you can send them to the banquette island to sort it out.

I love designing for Jeff + Amy, they often say things like "you're the boss" and trust every single suggestion I have. You have no idea how great it feels to have clients hire you and trust your vision. It not only makes my job ultra enjoyable it keeps the construction schedule going as there are always challenges that arise through remodeling where the design has to be tweaked. Even though they give me free reign most of the time, I work hard to check off all of their wants + wishes. This is their home and I want them to love every element.

the BEAUTY

technically serene

FAMILY ROOM

the WANTS the WISHES

It felt like there were more toys than carpet on the floor when I first stepped foot into Jeff + Amy's family room. Thank goodness they were not quite at the small LEGO stage yet as I am sure I would have walked away with an injury. We needed a solution to house Lyla + Cassie's toys in order to have the room function for their whole family. This is their main living area and is heavily used by all. They wanted a cozy, comfortable space with plenty of places to sit while having friends over, and allowing room for the kids to spread out and play.

the EVERYDAY

The room was all original other than the built-ins on either side of the fireplace which they had painted white. There were too many exposed shelves and the room felt cluttered. To solve that problem we added doors to the majority of the upper cabinets which worked great to tuck away games and toys. The fireplace needed some love so I sourced charcoal porcelain tiles, a honed hearth slab with a tumbled front and found reclaimed teak for the custom mantel. We added the wainscoting above the mantel to make the fireplace pop with all the new contrast.

In between the breakfast nook was the original oak railing, we adding a pony wall which allowed for custom toy storage. The room gets used a lot, and toys are constantly coming out of the cabinets and going back in, but everything has a place so it makes pick up very easy. The custom ottoman is a favorite space for the girls to play board games and spend time together.

The struggle in a room with a fireplace and a TV is that they are often competing for attention. The struggle is real. In a lot of cases the TV wins out. In this case we wanted to focus on the updated fireplace, not the TV. Jeff had plans for a 60" television and somehow I had to find a place for the TV while adding seating that would not block the view. Thankfully after Amy's initial shock of the daybed I proposed wore off, she warmed up to the idea. Now they have lots of seating for every activity. A favorite of Lyla + Cassie's the daybed is used for snuggling under blankets while watching a show or reading books together.

Jeff + Amy spend their evenings after the girls go to bed cozy on the sofa. Amy is either knitting or reading while Jeff plays on his laptop or flips on the TV.

I look forward to the day when I open my inbox and I see an email from Jeff + Amy as I have enjoyed every moment working with them, coming up with design solutions and solving construction problems. I suppose I will have to write another book to show you their stunning living room we recently finished! Stay tuned...

the BEAUTY

CUSTOM

When I first met Jeff + Amy there were multiple laptops and cords draped over the island a tad too close to their gas cooktop. This made me nervous to say the least. Since there was an open space at the end of their kitchen cabinets it only seemed fitting to have a freestanding piece made. I wanted it to feel different than the kitchen cabinets but still work with the design. We had the cabinet painted white with a beech butcher-block top and added casters so they can move it around if needed. Shallow drawers give laptops and tablets a place to go when not in use. We left enough space at the back of the cabinet to hold a power strip so all items could charge while snoozing away.

the HAPPY the SAD

I come from a corporate background. I worked for large international brands. The jobs we were doing in southern California and Seattle were the same jobs being done in Moscow and Tokyo, just with different outfits. As a cog in a big machine we were encouraged to follow the rules and to not step far out of the box. I knew what my days would be like. There were not too many surprises. It was not that things had become dull...okay, who am I kidding? I'm not a sit-behind-a-desk-all-day type of gal. I was stagnant and ready for something new.

During a brief introduction to the world of design and construction on my personal home remodel {what started as a bath remodel turned into a complete demo, rebuild and doubling the original square footage}, I decided I would like to learn more about interior design. I reached out to several designers offering my corporate marketing skills in trade for an intern position. I was willing to volunteer to find out if this was something I was interested in pursuing full-time. I received a few responses but the e-mail from Harmony just resonated with me. She was in the same town as me and her online portfolio was impressive. She was passionate about small business, {something I was longing to be part of} and not only did she think outside of the box, she tactfully kicked said box aside and created some of the most interesting designs full of reclaimed and custom items.

We met at a local coffee shop. I remember taking a phone call as I was walking across the street before the meeting. It was my husband wishing me good luck. He knew I could do whatever I set my mind to if given the opportunity.

In heels.
While pregnant.

Without his support I might not have taken the leap. Over lattes Harmony and I just clicked. A friend recently described us as opposites who balance each other out. What else could you ask for in a partner in crime, or design as the case may be? Harmony gave me the opportunity, I jumped two feet in while still working another full time job. I started on small projects for design-HARMONY behind the scenes including building online portfolios, website copy editing and "after" photo shoots for completed projects. Harmony's business was booming, I had a baby, she had a baby and then we were both ready for a full commitment.

And so begins the true journey.

Day 1 of my new project management role started with us meeting at a jobsite for a bathroom remodel already in process. Harmony wanted to go over design details after demo with our tile installer and double check the plumbing rough-ins. There was also the fact that a city inspector decided our jobsite was the one to pick on that week and delayed the project requiring additional inspections. So here I was, in the middle of a shell of a room, not sure exactly what was going on, and Harmony casually says, "Why don't you update the construction calendar, meet the inspector and verify the electrical placement for the vanity drawers?" Ummmm. Ok? I guess I never let on that I knew how to do exactly none of those things but with some trial and error and my friend Google, I was on the way to a finished bathroom. The phrase, "thrown into the deep end" rings a bell...Every day, I mean EVERY DAY I learn something new. I am faced with all types of personalities – from clients to contractors, to the customer service rep at Room & Board. No day is like the last. I would not have it any other way.

I think of a design project as a tree. Bear with me here folks.

A design, like a tree, starts with one seed. One kernel of inspiration that flourishes into a completed space. No two houses, like no two trees, are exactly alike. We never know what we are going to find when we start taking down walls.

I love demo day. I hate demo day.

Demo day means we open the walls, tear out the cabinets and create a blank canvas to create a totally re-imagined space. We now have blank walls to draw out our cabinet dimensions or appliance placement or where exactly we want outlets placed. This is also when we unfortunately find a vent pipe running smack dab in the middle of the wall we are removing, or electrical in need of a major overhaul. This means the construction calendar I so carefully planned will be extended until after Thanksgiving instead of having a kitchen ready to cook a big turkey dinner. The growth of our design tree is stunted, but only temporarily.

As much as I hate delays, I love problem solving. I get to work hand-in-hand with our trades to figure out the best alternative for the clients, being mindful of the costs but also the design. We get to lead our homeowners through the decision making process, offering solutions instead of dwelling on the problems. We are in the service industry so at the end of the day, if our clients are happy, we are happy.

Our trades are the sturdy trunk of our design tree. The strength of our relationships with these guys {yes, all of our onsite contractors happen to be men} forms the foundation for any project. For every phase of a project we have a different trade onsite – a team for demo and framing, another for electrical, another for plumbing and so on through to the final paint job. Our trades become like family as much, if not more, than our clients as we see them on multiple jobs on a daily basis.

There is one team of contractors that have always been kind and respectful towards me. Even when it was clear I had absolutely no idea what I was talking about, they patiently walked me through the options and solutions to any issues that may have arisen. About 8 months into working with them, we were demoing a master bathroom – remember how I love/hate demo day? One of the gentlemen was removing a wall of tile and it fell backwards towards him slicing his wrist down to the bone. My first thought was, "how do I get him out of here without dripping blood on our client's white carpet?". My brain quickly rushed to, "how fast can I get him to the ER?". His partner insisted on continuing to work – talk about work ethic – and I rushed off to the hospital with our poor client standing in the driveway with gauze {please note, no white carpets were ruined during this process}. I sat with him, talked with him and thought about how different my days had become since sitting behind a desk. Not boring, oh so not boring. Several stitches {18 I think} and a tetanus shot later, we were back on the jobsite and he was working with one hand. He wanted to make sure I stayed on track with my calendar! All of our partners are very important to us. Having well defined designs and the ability to communicate the construction specifics to several different personalities is key to my job. We might be the only ones in heels on a jobsite, but it is by our strong direction that the finished product comes together.

Eventually our tree branches and blooms. The final details come together down to the last light fixture hung or the last touch-up paint brushed. Our kitchens are ready for Christmas dinner and our bathrooms are ready for mom to escape in a luxurious tub.

Our clients are happy, but we are a little sad.

Much like fall when we enjoy the beauty of the changing leaves, there is also a little sadness that comes with the end of summer, or end of a project. We pull up the floor protectants and wipe up the drywall dust. We stage the room with pillows and accessories and add a vase overflowing with flowers. Then we set the keys on the counter, slip on our shoes and leave the project behind us. After months of daily communications with our clients and trades we are finished.

Done.

Until we get that call a few months later that their dining room could really use an update... and the seed is planted for yet another project. I am ready with my gloves and gardening shears for the next tree to grow.

- kate

The designs are only as good as the people who do the truly hard work and make them come to life. I can see it in my head. Then we must communicate all the details to the craftspeople we have come to depend on to make the vision reality.

Without all of them, we are just a whole lot of fluff.

our PARTNERS

{ in order of how we build out a room }

CARTER + STEVE
a dynamic duo of two studs

TODD
you make a pipe dream reality

PATRICK
consistently brightening our day

JOEL
you acclimate to our designs

YURIY + PAUL
detailed, dependable + forever flexible

MATT
soft spoken, soft close

MIKE
you are our rock, forever easing the edges

JACK
customizing our colors and design details

JULIE
you dress our rooms and keep us covered

CORY
you put the spotlight on our designs

two LEGS

four LEGS

about HARMONY WEIHS

A Pacific Northwest Native, Harmony was born and raised in Corvallis, Oregon with her parents and two sisters. In 1995 she moved to Seattle to study fashion design, and quickly became a true Seattleite obsessing over the perfect espresso.

Harmony left the corporate world of apparel design in 2006 to start designHARMONY as a freelance designer for apparel and bags in the outdoor industry. In 2009 she wanted to be more connected to the end user of her designs and started to transition into interiors. Though not formally trained in interiors, she built her business from the ground up, which was a challenging, ever changing task, but she has never looked back.

She is passionate about all things design, function and reclaiming materials to make one-of-a-kind designs. Harmony loves to have hands on experiences working with clients, trades and local craftspeople directly. She values supporting small, local businesses and being involved in her community.

Harmony resides in Kirkland, Washington with her 4 year old son Holden and 1 year old daughter Emma. Getting dirty in the garden planting her favorite vegetables, forever tweaking her recipes, and traveling is where you will find her when not living, breathing and dreaming all things design. Tickling and loving on her top two designs to date is where she feels most at home.

about KATE SAVITCH

Born and raised in the Pacific Northwest, Kate's passion for design translated into a career with her first job out of college, designing decor, planning and coordinating high-end corporate and social events in Southern California. She soon segued into all things real estate working to develop management and marketing strategies for some of the top builders and real estate agents in California and the Seattle area.

After building a custom home with her husband, Kate wanted to learn more about the design industry. Feeling stuck in her career, she reached out to several already successful designers in the area offering to intern or work on the side just to learn more about interior design. As luck would have it, Harmony replied to her inquiry and just like that, a partnership began that has blossomed into the designHARMONY of today.

A Washington native, Kate lives in downtown Kirkland, Washington with her business executive husband Keith, their 4 year old son Sam, 2 year old son Matt, third baby boy on the way and their dogs Norah and Ella. When not building sandcastles or train tracks with her boys, Kate can be found entertaining her large Seattle area family, reading a good book or searching for the perfect glass of cabernet.